LITTLE BOOK OF OK

BY

KY

MERMAID NURSE

Intro. to the Introduction

Have you ever wanted a book where you
read the ending first?

This is that book.

Go for it.

I dare you.

You never know,
the end could just be
the beginning in drag.

Just pick this book up,
ditch a hundred other things,
and bite into big hug nuggets.

Read any way you please.
Don' finish. Finish.
Read page fifty-two, fifty-two times.
It's ok. I don't mean ok in the
meaningless way tossed as trope.
I mean it as badass, transformational magic.

The voice of ok came to me in the midst of
a divorce, as the roof to my house caved in
after a storm. Fast forward to when
a drunk driver drove 50 mph off the road,
just missing the window where I stood, only to
plummet 160 feet off the bluff in my backyard.

I could go on, and so you could.
So much has happened and
keeps happening, doesn't it.

Make this book an **oasis of ok**. Please.

As you parooze the book, choose the voice Ok
talks to you in

A)   Ian Mckellen
B)   Marlene Dietrich
C)   Cate Blanchett
D)   Viggo
E)   Tom Waits

(Yes I'm biased toward LOTR where hobbits grow
ok in fields beside okra.)

Thank you to my children Arden and Chloe!

You've freed my kite from the tree with love and laughter over and over.

Unabashed Adoration

I dedicate this book to **you**
who appeared at just the right time.

Special shoutout to poets, oak trees,
nurses, kids, tapioca pudding,
and a cat named Mo who
made it perfectly ok, when it wasn't.
Thank you Gabriel my guitar
who's been with me since age 13.

I also want to acknowledge
the band **Ok Go**
and their amazing way of
saying it's ok
through music,
because music is the most
amazing ok.

Ecetera thank you's to

Kierra Schwab for the incredible cover illustration.
J. Beckman for the ink images.
Mandy Tran for being a badass patent attorney.
Faye Heimerl for taking me to the carousal of
happiness in the mountains and Quam Editing.
Ann White for Tails from the Enchanted Cottage.
Dr. Amy for resuscitating me with Florida breezes.
Fannie Weirauch for red sparkle wisdom.
Deb Sabo-Williams for your sunflower wisdom.
Elise Edmonds Cantrell for your encouragement
with 40 Days to Enlightened Eating.
Kelly Berrimen for turning your basement into
fairyland and dancing to 80's music on Fridays.
Mary Croy for your magpie poetry.
Ellen Crow Vodicka, for your yoga poetry.
Diane Valand, my faithful songbird.
Maria Flynn for One Wise Life, Mojo Mastery, and
loving the Lucille Ball in me. Steven Aitchison for
your inspiration and YDF.
Kyle Cease for deep down.
Christopher Witecki for your brilliant step
astrology and the Sirius Joy tribe oh I love you all
especially Joyce Sweeney, Jill Miffler, Kim Jankow
LeRoy, Valarie Marks, Pamela Haythe...

Introduction

When's the last time you felt ok

yesterday,
ten years ago,
never?

If you haven't answered today
get to it and
check your sock drawer, the sky, your
friend's smile,
and this book.

What if
being ok
could be a source of undiscovered
huge energy.

What if
ok is really a

superpower!

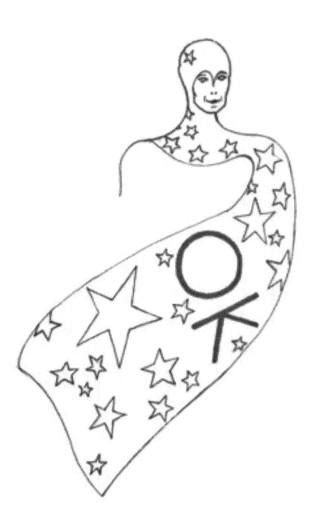

What if I told you I'm a nurse who's really a
mermaid and
I have a map
to lead you to a treasure
so rich
so simple
it gives you a wealth of health and
pleasure today!
As a nurse and mermaid, I'm here to help
you find pragmatic ways to be ok
and access happiness
after the tragedy of heartbreak.

Being human isn't easy.

You know this.
Perspectives shift on a penny.

Suddenly, you feel safe
despite chaos, pain, lutefisk.

I found a way to feel ok at age 25,
shaking from a 7.1 earthquake
in San Francisco.

If you choose inFINcible perspective,
a mysterious resiliency can change
deadlines to lifelines.

You say its not easy?
Is it really easier to not be "ok"?
Be okay and
stuff you love
will come to you.
I hope Lao Tzu is laughing
as I say that my mermaid way.
Hundreds of years ago he said
"Be really whole and all things will come to
you".

When insurance plans fail,
ok will be a mantra
candling the dark.

Feel warm, content, and
extravagant.
Have enough ok.

Please pass the ok gravy
to the person next to you.

The world

needs

more

ok.

I

Are you Ok?

Hi.

I'm the little book of ok

and
I say to you
beautiful goofball

it's
going to be
ok.

Right?!
I hear you cough coffee.
(space for your coffeesplat)

It's going to be ok because
I'm stubborn and say so.
I've survived over 175 years
since that first cool cat
said ok in two letter form.

I was here prior to that in
spills, bullsh*t, tragedy,
and pistachio shells.

So no matter what happens

I'll stay awake with you, baby.
During 3 a.m. heartbreak.
I'll take you there
where it's ok.

And on days without a hat,
when you're out'a chocolate,
and alone,
I'll be here
with a kiss
whispering dear one, it's ok.

How is it possible
that I kiss you with ok?
Because, I believe in you
like sunlight believes in you.

I wake your face with
golden rays
everyday, saying rise
fill your eyes with sky!

I want this for you.
I've missed your smile.

Please be inspired and
a bit silly. Surprise
yourself once in a while.

Kick back with ok.

Out of the blue
say ok and do it,
whatever it is for you.

Don't miss out.

Did you realize that was me
decadently laying ok
on you, dear one?

Or have you chosen
my doppelgänger "not ok"
one too many times and struggled,
instead of snuggling up to
plush ok.

Haroompf, that's ok, I'm here
now. I won't give up on you.

**Let me puppy jump
leap on your lap!**

Woooooooooooooooosh!

Time to splash your
keister with ok.

Forget those dirty dishes and
dance with me
sashay shoop.

Drop it like it's hot
to quote Great Aunt Pearl.

Be the King or Queen of ok.
(you choose who you are)

You dream of it being easier,
don't you darling,
even special,

a "night at the museum"
kind of life where
someone lets you in,
gives you
extra consideration,
and
most
of
all
notices...

you

are

wonderful!

Get ready for what's next.

Why settle for anything less?

Ok is the best!!!
if I do say so myself as
Grandma Dorothy Ella Henrietta
used to say.

So boast and toast ok!!!

Because you know what?

Ok is even better than yes!

Because YES is a
know it all sassy pants who
seldom delivers due to
overscheduling.

Instead...

OK IS SPECTACULAR

paving the way to
love, adventure, and
your ability to create
the life you want!

Ok is strange efficiency.

Just
lay back,
locate that cozy spot,
and love what you love.

Watch
sh*t happen **shazam**
from this relaxed place.

Let's face it, ok
is snazzy like a cracker
and crunchy fun.

Please, have another ok cracker
and continue.

Why do I give you crackers and
kiss you wicked with

ok?

Because dearest,
you are right,
life isn't a fairytale
but you know what

ok has the velocity
to shake angels awake
and make today
off the charts
terrific great.

Deep breath.

And it has pragmatic magic
the earthquake kind,
able to shift teutonic plates
of all you want, dream, need,
with
the next breath.

Breathe with me.

Say outloud on the outbreath
in the most beautiful moviestar
way

...o
...k

And another
delicious breath...ok....

Know that the energy of
ok is nothing less than
the fire of life
overflowing from a
a love volcano.

Gawk at its freakin' strength
as it revives all in its path,
expanding happiness.

Give yourself over to
its mythic mountaintop and
somersault to tommorrow
yodel'n oooooooo-k.

Or don't yodel, that's ok.

Sense the energy of ok
surge through earth,
west wind to waterfall,
rolling down the
bowling alleys of your very veins.
(not sorry about that last one)

Fill the next minute with
gobs of ok.

Feel it begin
to glisten
as if
bird-bursting from
scrunch of eggshell.

Gallyoompf into
the new day.

Get going.
Do it.
With or without
a jacket.

I don't mean to speak strangely
as if I'm an ancient, gypsy dousha.
I admit I do so to get your
attention because I'm so
often overlooked.
I'm often thought of as
that old gray sweater
oversized, with spilled oatmeal
stuck to a button.

Please don't misunderstand.
I didn't abandon you
in your sadness
that day you thought I'd left.
No. I approached,
pulled up a chair,
spanakopita in my cheek and

said with a velvety voice

SOKEHSHHHH:OK

You didn't understand.

How could you.

But I never left.

Please don't forget,
that despite entropy,
it's all right
inside and out,
beneath, beside, above.

Ok is a sweet wink
so needed as the world implodes
with poverty, war, and pain.
When you see despair
everywhere let me care for you.
I come to you
unarmed to hold you in my arms.

I'm here to take your heavy heart
to Paris with this promised kiss.
I beckon come out of trepidation
and depression. Soar.
I've opened the cage door.
You no longer need small spaces.
Never did.

Precious creature,
meant to stretch with
every bit of imagination and
passion possible....

I believe in you so!

The door is open.
The light is on.
Potatoes are simmering.
Get ready to slather them with

OK GRAVY.

Then, nestle in
for the night.
I'll tuck you ok.

Come morning
forgive everything.

Travel light.

I'll carry you to safety,
lift you by the scruff.

Yup, I'm that
ninja cat mama and

I've gotcha.

So breathe deeper
and please
read on.

**You won't believe
what I'm about to say...**

2.

Ok is a magnificent way to take care of yourself.

You don't want much,
do you.

Love. Umbria.
A brain that remembers.
A train ride through the
mountains. Tiramasu.
Health. Wealth.

And

maca-ok-damia nuts!

Most of all
you want
to feel ok.

Well, it's time.

Hear it, see it,
taste and touch it
my dovecote,
because it's the
flavor of the day!
Have a huge scoop of ok
and feel better!

Call me Doctor Ok.
When I'm in the house,
you don't need to
call the other doctors
as often because
I'm
amazing.

Pssst, I'll tell you a secret...

...an ok a day
keeps the other ones away,
because I lower blood pressure,
ease your heart, and feed
you fabulous, fresh organic ok.
Yummmm.

Dr. Ok costs just one thing.

You must
give up
"not ok".

That's it.

Onions and butter you say!?!

Listen, if you
try to outrun your tears or
stuff them behind your nose,
soon a sniffle will swell into a
sinus infection and drip
down
as you drown in a tsunami
you didn't cry.

This happened to a dear
fifty year old woman in
New Orleans who didn't
cry after a heartbreak because she
said she was too busy, but then
disaster happened.

I can't emphasize enough
how vital it is to reboot
to ok. Don't you want to
make room for all you
need, feel, and dream?

Breathe.
Heave ho, let go
follow the flow of tears.
Look through this
iridescent, pearly world
and cry. Don't be surprised
when from behind tired eyes...

A GLOW HAPPENS

as
happiness springs up
from sadness
because you chose ok.

Do something right now.

Don't
think of that
one hurtful thing
you've been thinking of
all day and take a deep breath.
HA got ya!

As you breathe out,
give that pain a color
and blow it away

kerpoof!

Breathe in again and feel
a pink polkadot blanket of ok
suddenly appear beneath
your chin as you curl up to nap.

Sweet sassafras!

Wake day after day with
a huge hug from ok
horizon to horizon.

Get ready, get set, glow!

Have a cup of sun.

Nibble on this simple minute.

Taste today!

**Be astonished
and
sense energy
rush in with**

sexy, self-acceptance
**where no one's at fault,
all is forgiven,
and you and I smile
at nothing in particular.**

La de da ok?!

Pitterpat to this simple

picnic of ok

**no rush, push, crash
only flow
of ok.**

**And you know what
the crazy amazing
thing is?**

Ready for this?

When

you start meeting others who
follow the flow and glow of ok

suddenly

it's as if
the room

begins

to

shine

bright supernova style.

Each ok lights up
and takes its place
in a constellation
of Sirius ok.

Then, guess what!
You start to hear music as if
you're in your own movie
vibing with various levels of ok.

Watch stuff get real
as you leap like a child
in love with little and big things.

Heart cartwheeling
singing freely with a frequency
sweet corn to treetop.

Turn your world
further with more ok
despite war, suffering,
sickness, and hunger.
Whirl past hurt
with a perspective to
live invincible.
(inFINcible
as a mermaid would say)

Let me share another
survival secret. You and I
know pain daily.
There's no escaping it.
But grasp this—
suffering is
different from pain.

You may not be able to
control or stop pain, but
you choose to suffer, or not.
Your response to pain
determines the suffering.
Let me say it another way.
Pain happens and
you and I feel it.
Yet
through passionate
detachment and patience,
whether that's stretching,
meditation, breathing,
you and I can reach
a place of ok.

Capiche?

Don't make me come over there
and slap your self-pity like a
gypsy dousha grandma with
great love.
Enough nonsense of this not ok.
I tell you, **it's ok**
and there are
butterscotch stars to
touch with your tongue.
OK!

Doesn't matter if
a doozy of a problem
is tucked in your back pocket.

Reach out with your empty
hand and understand

you are stardust.
Trust all that funny lust.
Light every candle you can.

Sing, laugh, eat a piece of cake,
even though it's not
your birthday.
Ok is a great way to be
happy, healthy,
and yes horny.
Ok is an aphrodisiac.

So get naked with lanky ok.
Celebrate with someone you love

cirque du ok!

Ok is a way
to feel free
and see who
you really are.

Tip upside down and
double dip
glimpse from
another view.

Ooze ok
all over you.

Just imagine, what will happen

when you've eaten enough
sweet, wicked ok

**topped with spectacular sprinkles
of ok, per protocol.**
(feel free to draw sprinkles of ok
in the space below)

**"Freedom is a breakfast food"
e.e. cummings the poet wrote.
He probably ate pancakes
droozled with maple ok
mmmmmmmmm.**

**Be right back
I'm going to go eat a
pancake, ok?**

**Mmmmmm
yummmmmm
want some
mmmmmmm
imaginary pancakes
they are amazing!**

**Ok, I've put the magic spatula
down. Don't be daunted when
others can't understand
and doubt your sanity.
Let them laugh.**
**(sadly they haven't tried
imaginary pancakes)**

**Don't get defensive, rather ask
them to pass the lingonberries.**

Yes, it's your inherent right to
risk looking like an idiot.
Promise me you'll never
apologize for your pizazz.

Anyone who believes in ok
understands it has magic
and plants a lavender path
in the center of anxiety.

Add a basket with
six kittens, if you wish.

Ok is magic
packed with
creative **oomf**

the kind that launches
rockets and rhapsodizes
with stars.

So go get a scissors and
make a paper snowflake out of
that receipt stressing you out.
Be silly and insist it's ok.
Whistle while you
grocery shop. Pay the bill
for the person behind you.

Travel to Iceland and
dump the bucket list
over your head.
Shiver and live!

Don't be afraid.

Be crazy brave with

big ok!

Excavate ok.
Go after it with
sand shovel, spatula,
lotsa hootspa, and finally
fall off the couch with a friend
laughing for no reason.

Smile.
Be a horizon someone will fly to.

Soon smiles spread for miles
as the world becomes more ok.

(Please draw swooping, swirling,
spiraling smiles on the back of a cat
or all over this book)

The next time
someone doesn't see
your smile and they walk away
though you loved them,
just jump in the lake.
I'm not kidding.

Dive deeper.
You are love which is
a different thing
than you are loved.

**FINd the starry arc in your story!
Lift from
victim to inFINcible.
(mermaid innuendo)**

**You can be anything
anytime
when you deFINe your shine.**

**So
no matter what
know
you've got this!**

**Right now
I'm giving you
a ticket to**

cosmic ok!

FINd rich, wide sky.

Defy.
Parasail over problems.

You're able to do this
because

ok has magical activation ability.

It does.
Be blown away

WOOOOOOOOOOOOSH

be amazed at today.

It's vivid with
blue vista breakthrough
and berry patch.

Ride a carefree bicycle
over open roads.
Taste ok on honeysuckle breezes.

Go to
the Galapagos or the
living room of the one you love
with a backpack full of OK.

Plunk down
in the
middle of
an ordinary
moment
where you
are a hero
of ok

which is
all you
really have
to do.

That. And

stay spontaneous
about
all
the katywampus ways
ok brings it.

Do another cool thing.

When life falls apart
go to
the center of your
heartache.
Take the pieces.
Lift them to the light.
Turn them around
till they're a **hopescope**
of what broke!

See things
    the   unique way
        you   do.
    It's your truth.

Stay strong
in a world of naysayers.
who think it's a joke
when you say it's ok.

One day, they may sneeze and see
everything is ok in the end.
This happened to my Uncle Ed
who raised his fist
at postmen and kids,
then one day, he didn't.

Old stories do die,
characters who clamor
'complete me' will stop.
So for now, just be ok
and don't let anyone take it away.

Walk away without knowing
where you're going.

Know,
it's ok if
you don't know
where you're going,
most don't.

If you get lost
just laugh or whistle,
do both at same time if you can.

If you don't recognize
where you are,
it's because

it's beautifully new
and you are being true
to your heart, searching for
a freer way.

Know though you feel lost,
the trees see you.
Just breathe and

keep ok-ing!

You may be accused of not
having a plan,
and when that happens,
don't be discouraged

keep on ok'ing!

Let go of what was never yours.
It's of little use now.

Don't get pressed to the horizon
by
abuse and judgement

just keep ok'ing!

Put pain down
for a minute
and see what happens.

A sudden happiness
may come up and offer
a yellow umbrella.

Toss penny memories of lost loves
into a fountain and
suddenly find
you keep them
better this way.

Discover love you forgot
in empty pockets
beside acorns and agates,
and go your merry way.

The hour is a flower.
It's fragrant
with
the chance
to choose something different!

A lallapalooza
of love
wants to
burst through the
winter in your heart.
Remember
planting that dapper seed.
Yes? No? Maybe so!

You were eight and
late for something
but it didn't stop you.

You knew a lucid moment
as you spied your future self
in a puddle you thought
to be a portal.

You believed
in a
happy, extravagant ok
in that moment of abandon,
even though they'd abandoned
you.

You intuited
an escape route to a
safer place.

You climbed a spiral staircase
through
cerulean architecture of heart to
where you arrived and
stand right now alive
breathing stars.

And now at three a.m.
a cat sits in
an open window
purring a
phenomenal ok.
Welcome
this stray
back home.

Be like a kid
and begin again,
though you feel old.

Believe
with your
next breath

ok is a kite

reminding you
to
rise above
limitation and fear.

Prioritize the sky
and let it inspire you
as you die in slow holiness
like a sunset
because you are dying
and that's ok too.

3

Ok is a way to make peace in the world from my Ky heart to yours.

Remember
when
you put a shell to your ear
and heard the sea?
Then, clunk,
you understood it wasn't
the sea?
Did your heart sink?
Mine did. Then I thought,
wait.
The blood beating inside me,
is the same
starlight and saltwater.
Isn't it,
except
it's called electrolytes and saline.

Everywhere
unexplainable tenderness,
mistaken transcendence,
and incandescent spit.

Seize this chance to swim
past disappointment.

Go out the front door and
head to class, but pause
with awe, as it hits—
that what you're really doing is
dancing across the planet.

Realize this remarkable
fact and defy with a smile,
that could be hiccups.

Persist.
Squint if you must.
Make an appointment
at noon with the muse.
If she doesn't show,
shrug, take the bus,
and find what you need,
eavesdropping on the folks
three rows back.

Keep discovering
it's something
just to be alive.
There's something
to love in all of it.

Ok offers a unique frequency
to tune in to
galactic ok.

Ok attracts more ok.

It's pb and jelly physics.

When you
choose to be ok,
you believe the
best intention
of what's possible.
This creates...
wait for it
whoa....
a mobius of possibility!

So crank the music, baby.
Sing along to Ok Go's
video "This too shall pass".
Tumble somersault
to anything by Ok Go.

Growl with Joe "Feeling all right".
Linger with Annie Lennox and
a 'A Thousand Beautiful Things".
Croon "Don't worry about a t'ing"
with Marley and all the birds in
the world. Turn the day around as
you cry for joy to Coldplay's "Every
Tear a Waterfall". Top it off with
Sigur Ross and look up at the sky.
Sing with Sting "Brand New Day".

When it finally grows quiet
and you're alone in a crowd
and no one looks you in the
eye, look yourself in the eye
in the nearest sunglass rack
and wink.

It's documented from grandmas
to astrophysicists, that the axis
in the room will shift because
of this quintessential wink.

Soon, you'll be eating pizza,
laughing rootbeer
out yo' nose, and
singing till the place closes,
because of the epic wink.

Once that's done,
something incredible
can happen.
You'll have the
ability to listen to
someone else
so deeply,
it's as if
you're suddenly a dolphin
able to echolocate
a place you both can feel ok.

(Imagine a dolphin leaping through
waves of okay in the space below)

Hone in on ok
and show up
for another
effortlessly.
It's a way
of coming home
from a lonely moment.

Say "you're ok"
and make someone a neighbor.

Ok makes room
on the street, at the diner,
in the theater, at the beach.

Soon there's laughter in the aisles,
and

by the
pie carousal.

When you tell someone

you're ok

it's a way of saying
I respect you
not just for
what you do,
but for who you are.
who you are
who you are
who you are............you are...

(enjoy the echo,
you're in a canyon of ok)

If you choose to be ok,
nationalism, religion,
gender, and sex,
melt into a global ok
where war, poverty,
and starvation decrease,
because ok makes peace
and transforms suffering.

Ok wakes daily
takes down greed by
sharing what's needed and
then sharing even more.
Ok is so generous,
it generates fresh energy,
enough to feed countries,
whales, and angels.

Know
when it's withheld,
it endangers places
needing love.
When
naysayers say, it's not ok,
a bomb is dropped on
territory that could've been ok.

Be the **hulk of ok**.

Stand by what you love.
Take down conflict,
not with a dagger,
but with swag and a hug.

I'm hugging you right now,

with sooo much ok
it's ergonomic for your
uhganomic.

Stop fighting a battle
that doesn't matter
the way you think it does.

Stahhhhp.
You've already won.
Do a victory dance
beside the little book of ok.

When you choose to be ok
you're a mountain
others come to, to watch the
gold sunrise.

Ok gives stability,
dignity, intimacy,
and the chance to travel light.

Ok is miraculous,
changing things
with faith which
makes it dangerous.

Be the **dojo** of
ok mojo.

Be badass ok
and take down bullies
in your mind,
at the office, on the playground.

Offer
this simple soup, thumbs up.

You don't have time to be cruel,
because you're too busy doodling
and crooning "Le Mer"
which washes away hate.

When you feel you can't go on
ok blows up a floatie
during sea change.

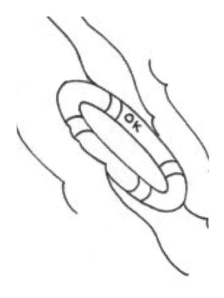

Did you know
The Navajo/Diné
believe in the
Beauty Way
which blesses east to west,
within, without,
and then some.

Yes, let the beauty of ok
also bless every direction.
The beauty of ok
hovers with love
above us, below us,
before, beside, and
within.

Hear your own heartbeat

say O-K

O-K

O-K

O-K

O-K

The reality is
you and I are a
human heaven on earth.

We're able to love
what we love
without shame or blame.

Our sweet, salty spirit has
fingertips and lips.

Take it in...

ahhhhhhhhhhhhh

and not only that...

ok makes it possible to
accept
rather than repent,
feel
rather than rationalize,
remain
rather than escape.

Ok makes an offer
you cannot refuse,
a warm wamdoozle,
wonderful with
wholeness.

(isn't "w" just the letter to hold all that ok
raining down?! Draw a few and see if they fly
off the page like birds)

The grace of ok
takes one beyond
sin or guilt. It doesn't let
bad advertisements
interrupt the
lovestory.

Not one bit.

Are you tired of
feeling you have to tweak a
corner, take a pill, and achieve
more, because
"they" say so?

Repeat after me
there's no 'they'
there's only this ok. (repeat)

Few places remain
where the you are not ok
lie isn't sold to us. Some
priests, doctors, dictators
claim we're lazy, sick, weak,
and worse, because they're not
working the ok.

The biggest heist in history
is the same one that keeps
happening. It's the one
that aims to take ok away.
Driven by the need to control,
it comes from greed
which comes from fear.

What if
you and I
let go of fear.

Would an afternoon breeze
take us to a table tonight
by the lapis sea as
an Italian waiter asks
who ordered the easy breezy caprese

and you'd smile
and say I did,
because you're
done with the struggle.
It's time for salad
because ok is sacred
like a tomato.
Yes.
enjoy the extravagance
of ok, as it spills in basil,
balsamic pools of olive oil.
Enjoy easy breezy caprese ok.

This is
the wealth the health
meant for you
get giddy rich with it!

This moment of ok is worth more
than anything else on the shelf.

Be ok
in ways that can't be explained.
The law of ok is deeper
than the law of physics.

This is because
the law of ok is written by
life itself, and is life itself
even in death.

No matter what happens,
hurricane or haggis,
it can be ok.

Yes, this million dollar
enigma in a brown bag of ok
befuddles, doesn't it?

How can it be ok
when the world hurts
and you bleed on blue sky days.

As a nurse, I've helped, held,
fed, heard, cleaned, and
closed the eyes of those who died,
while loved ones cried.

I saw how lovers
travel light
in and out of
the horizon in each other's eyes.

The wide sky
of ok, made a way
to defy gravity.

Awe and awful
sat side by side
agreeing to disagree.

And you know what else?
When you and I remember
to take a deeper breath,
a safer place surfaces
despite the pain.
It's as if

Ok becomes oxygen!

Swimming the mystery of
this...
turned a hospice nurse to a
mermaid nurse. I learned to
deal with the depth of everything
as if breathing underwater
navigating the great
terrible beauty of life.

What is this life
where laughter
dances with grief?
Where less is more.
What's lost is found
and the finite minute
becomes infinite?

The greatest truths cannot be
grasped by the mind,
because the mind can only
think in opposites.
Instead, you and I must
listen with the heart
to this koan of ok
sung by the sea.

Swim mystery
with the honesty of
the heart, that surpasses
what the mind can grasp.

Please dear one, breathe.
It's really ok no matter what you
lose or choose.

Swing between ok and not ok, as if
you've found a hammock in your
heart on an island by the sea.
Go there often.
Never leave.

As you rock this hammock
realize you are safe
in your **oasis of ok.**

You may even FINd
you're a mermaid,
able to love and move
through simultaneous worlds
of happiness and sadness,
but more on that in my next book
Secret Mermaid Stuff.

**For now, show up today
with a warm, delicious ok.**

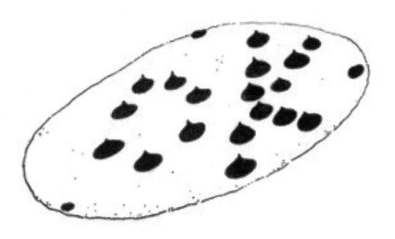

**Eat it,
break it,
and give peaces away.**

Comfort someone,
most of all yourself,
with this homemade ok.

Gulp it with a cup of sun
and never give up.

You are always closer
to ok than you could
ever imagine.

Be amazed as pain
melts away to the point where
only music remains.

Ok my love?

OK!

(go ahead, you know you want to
draw a smiley face inside the O)

Made in the USA
Las Vegas, NV
10 May 2021